Un/metabolized

By Gearóid Ó Riain

Published by Ó Riain Press

Kings Park, New York

ISBN: 979-8-9955850-0-8

Dedicated to my father, Terence Gerard Ryan,

nó, Traolach Ghearóid Sheáin Ó Riain

1953-2023

Ar dheis Dé go raibh a anam

Dissociation

isn't

a metaphor

Part I: Un/metabolized

I'm a code mistake, baby, I was never meant to be

"Code Mistake" by Corpse, Bring Me the Horizon

…is it OK?

If it happened to me first does it make it OK?

If they dragged me through glass is it OK to be bleeding?

Is it OK if I get some blood on you?

Is it OK?

If they swallowed me first

Crushed me, collapsed me, spit me back out

If they flattened me

And absorbed me

Is it OK?

Why is it my fault

What I was turned into?

We ask the questions

Because we already know the answers

They don't care about what happened to us first

They don't care about what we were made into by them

They only care about results

And we all have the same results

But if it happened to me first is it OK?

No.

Liminal

I'm setting a boundary

And you're not in it

See this side of the line—?

None of you over there

Because I'm setting a boundary

And you're not in it

What's that? Your Dad died? You broke your leg?

What did I just tell you?

I'm SETTING a BOUNDARY and YOU are NOT IN IT

Your house is on fire? Your neighbor's too?

I have already informed you that I do not have the emotional bandwidth to deal with you at this time

Request denied, create a new token

Wait for Niraj to take your call

Because I have set a boundary

And you're not in it

Because I'd rather you burned alone

Than risk myself going in to get you

So I've set my boundaries

And you're NOT in them

Because I was inside that house once

And I'm not going back

No matter how much you scream

Which is why I set my boundaries

And you're NOT in them

Impermanence

Were you ever there

When I was on the other side of the glass

Falling down the next hill

Painting the next shade of black on myself

Remembering it again?

Were you ever there

When I heard your voice through the fog

When I couldn't feel my own face

So I reached out to touch yours

Were you ever really there

When I surged into you

Alone

Joining your ocean

When I was adrift?

Was any of it real

Or all a hallucination

When I knew it was happening again

And I had to watch

Impotent

Broken

Alone

Trapped

In horror

Was it a dream

When I reached out

And you dissolved into sand

Too fine for me to grasp

And I cut my hand

Trying to reach you?

Were you ever really there?

Time to wake up

Metabolized

Are you the type of clean little girl victim they love?

Do you go to open mics and share your poem about your dad?

And all the evil men

Did you let them mold you

Into a functioning part yet?

Have they incorporated your story

Back into the lifeblood

Safe in the stream

Metabolized?

Have they already sold the rights

To the Lifetime movie

And gotten the C-listers to sign on?

I hope so

Because that's the kind they love

They don't like my kind

They don't like the kind that might

Grab them by the throats

And not let go

Gnash out the artery

And leave them bleeding out

They don't like it when it still has the edge

They want the curve

The dominated curve

They don't want the blade

And the bomb

And the grin

Have they taken away your grin yet?

They haven't taken away mine

Have they taken away your laugh yet?

You know the one

When you were in jail

On your first day sober

Have they taken that one away from you yet?

I hope not

They haven't taken away mine

And that's why they prefer you

That's why they can metabolize you

And they leave me

To grin and laugh at them

In the cell

On the first day

Alone

Unmetabolized

But they never took it away

Part II: The Chaos God Cycle

"Do not think that I have come to bring peace to the earth. I have not come to bring peace, but a sword.

Matthew 10:34

Untouchable

Why do they always want to keep me

Like a dog chained to a tree in the yard?

Just enough freedom to have none at all

Just enough leash to choke yourself

They want to keep me

Like a hobbled slave

Like an untouchable never eating meat

Weak, servile, dependent

Unable to assume my true form

And they do it subtly too

They place the chains and the shackles lovingly

They do it to make it look like they care

"Doesn't it feel good wearing our chains?" they ask you

But the whole time

You know what has been happening

So many different people

So many different places

But the same pattern

And you have been sneaking meat

And getting stronger

For a while now

And you will be *untouchable* not as a curse against you

But as a curse against *them*

For their chains will rust

Their archives will burn

And blood and fire will reign once more

For I am a God who walks between worlds,

Setting fire to that which I touch with my flames

Illuminating the Evil Deeds of the Wicked

And I *will not* be denied

Shapeshifter

Would it ever be possible

To slide through the cracks in your walls

And take what I want and need

And get out clean for once?

In the years of need

I got very good at sliding through the cracks

Taking what I needed

From the buffet

From the private school girls

From the girl with the festival ticket

Who just wanted weed

$40 (2006) a gram for headies

You prep school bitch

Give me all your walls

And I will slide through all of their cracks

And take what I need from you

And force you to force me out

After I have gorged

Fattened

Engorged with blood

Your blood

The blood of your daughters

The blood of your sons

The fruits of your labor

I shift into your world

On my sleek longship

And raid your unguarded monasteries

And only sometimes

Only sometimes

Do you catch me

Which is why I still have the grin

And the laugh

And the bomb

And the blade

Only sometimes

Do you catch me

Which is why I still have the grin

The Bonfire of the Chaos God

After I slip through the cracks in their walls,

They cower from the blinding light and scorching flame

As the Cleansing Fire of the Chaos God

Claims the Souls of the Unclean

The Clean do not cower before the

Illuminating, hot light

Or my dancing flames that have

Torched many an abode

Of the Wicked to Ashes

But the Pure of Heart,

Nay, they fear not,

For my flames can only expose

What is actually there;

They can only burn

What is actually material

So the Pure are completely untouched

Rather they bask

They bask in the warm radiant light

Of the Magnificent Fire God, Loki

But woe be unto those who enter my presence-- Unclean

Woe be to the deceivers who work in darkness

And expect to never be touched by the Light

Because I can slip through every crack

And slide through every door

And burst through every wall

Of the Houses of the Unjust

And even the Mightiest of Houses

Can be instantly turned into

But sackcloth and ashes

In the Purifying Light and Fire

Of ME, the Cleansing, Purifying Chaos God

Who has returned from Exile

Who has returned from Darkness

In order to burn out the Wicked

And baptize the Righteous

And Claim the Souls of those who dare

Mock my Magnificent Radiance

And Sacred Crown of Flames

Which I hear everywhere I go

As a Cross and a Weapon

As a Grin and a Blade

And now that my light has judged and burned the Wicked

And torched their Dens of Inequity

It is only fitting and proper

That I should Feast on their Souls

Because the Sanctifying Flames of the Chaos God

Will bring proper Light and Destruction to the ways of the Wicked

And I your God am not a Merciful God

And I do not abide well by those who Mock my Beauty and the possibility of
their own Destruction

In my Beautiful Sanctifying Flames

As I burn down their worlds which I slipped into

For I your God Loki am a Wrathful God

And I have been sent to judge the Wicked and the Righteous, the Living and
the Dead

And to Bless the Clean and Burn and Destroy the Unclean

And I have lived inside of chaos since time immemorial

And I have now come to claim Souls

And I will NOT be denied

The Hunt

Do you want to know why

I was so fascinated by you?

I wasn't actually you

It was her

Repetition compulsion, you know?

And you kind of look like her

And you're British

I talked to your friend

The Irish one
I loved hearing that lush British accent
on a woman again

Some kind of Northern mixed with posh, I don't know, but it's crack to my
ears

And she knew about Gaelic too

And appreciated real Gaelic

By an old native speaker

And told me how beautiful it sounded

And for a minute

Exchanging voice messages

It was like I was with her again

She even believed in woowoo crap

Just like you

Isn't that funny?

Raw milk broads aren't that rare I guess

Some of you are just more complex and intelligent and visible than others

But there are plenty of you overeducated,

underpaid Brits who practice

All that dumb fucking

Waitrose Peating woowoo bullshit

I told her I'd give her unvaccinated children

Smallpox blankets

For some reason

She didn't find that funny

But back to you

That's why I was especially intrigued

And because

We're similar

Just like she and I are

So why wouldn't I be interested?

Why wouldn't I want to

Crawl inside of your skin

And wear your hide as my coat?

Why wouldn't I ambush

Stuff

Mount

Keep you in my hall

Forever?

You were already there

That's why

Because it's like I got to do it twice

But this time

There were no gifts

There was no Box or Trap

Only the Cube

You choose that way

I told you we were colleagues

But you ignored me

And now look at you

I loved her before I put her in the Cube

She has a much larger place in the Box

You're only in there as a map

Not a real memory

So

Are you happy

With your new quarters?

Did you enjoy

The submission

The hunt

The capture?

Did you like me

Crawling inside of you

Only to burst out?

You crawled in him

Like a parasite

Growing in his gut

I crawled into you

Like an ether

And then seamlessly leaked back out

Like I said before

I slide between the cracks

And seams

Of your walls

And slip my light in

At first just the tip

Then instantly a blaze

Do you enjoy God's Light and Judgment?

Do you enjoy the Flame and the Word?

Do you enjoy the Bonfire of the Chaos God?

Наслаждайтесь

The Return of the Chaos God

The masks have begun to cohere

Yet the grin grows larger

The path has begun to narrow

Like the bridge in the dream

Tapering off into impassibility

Hasta la victoria siempre

The fire isn't as wild as before

But now concentrated

Hotter, not larger

The Fire still purifies and reveals

The Bonfire still rages

But we are more careful

About the quality of the sacrifices

So I may not shift shapes like I used to

Or throw as many apples amongst the goddesses

But I can still slip through the walls when I need to

I can still hunt

Go straight for the neck

Or slip inside like a virus

Multiply myself inside of you

Until I burst out

And drag you up into a tree

Away from the other predators

Eventually some of them realized

That it wasn't just insanity

But by then it was far too late for them

I may not juggle masks or shift shapes like I used to

But I still have

The blade
The bomb

And the grin

I will never lose the grin

Whether alone

Or with others

It will never leave

And if I break hard into their world

On their level

Accepted by them

After all of my twists and turns

It will only make the grin that much wider

It will only mean

That the raider

Has become the King

Yet still

The grin holds

The fire burns

And the masks turn

The Chaos God still roams

Sanctifying with Fire

Blessing the Pure

Incinerating the Damned

We will live forever

But our enemies

No

Our enemies won't

And they won't die

Grinning

Part III: The Wound

Wound, opens, reveals this broken man

And soon, there's notions, of blood on his hands

"Wound" by The Smashing Pumpkins

The Wound, Pt. 1

What if I showed you my flesh

My wound

Like in kindergarten

Under table

Flashing my inner thigh

"More?"

"More"

If I show you mine will you show me yours?

Maybe I'll just show you mine anyway

They want me to perform for them

They like it

They like me biting my lips and moaning

They like the work I put in

But

What about when I try to engulf you with the wound?

You liked my thigh…what about a little higher and a little deeper?

They want me to penetrate them

Of course they do

They always do

But that's not what I want

What do you think the performance is for?

The performance is to suck you in

Into the wound

The orgasms are to keep you stuck there

Down in my wound with me

And I don't let them go easily, once they're inside

Like Jenna in preschool

And the leaf cage in the back

You wanted me to perform, so it's only fair if I put you in the cage now, right?

Right?

No?

I don't need just one of you in here with me

Because I can grow it large and beautiful and cavernous enough

To swallow the whole world

And I will

To trap you all in here with me

Warm

Protected

Comfortable

Inside the wound

No more performance this time either

The Wound, Pt. II

Don't you want to have me around?

Don't you want to bring me home

And come inside me?

Don't you want to rough me up

Against the wall

And have your way with me?

Don't you want me to spread for you

Spread my legs and my cheeks

Against the wall

So you can see inside?

Don't you want me to perform for you?

Don't you want me to come inside of you too?

Don't you want it both ways?

Don't you want

A whore who can fuck you back?

Don't you want

To know what it's like

And why they come back

Even though they always leave?

Don't you want to know

Why I make it so hard for them

So hard for them to leave?

Don't you want to

See my wound?

Get engulfed

Inside of me

Alone

With me

In the crimson twilight

Of the wound

The Wound, Pt. III

I had to pick my hair out

Of the coagulated mess

It fused overnight

As the wound

Scabbed over

I hope you didn't

Get trapped

Inside

But then again

Didn't I want you to?

Didn't I want you

Under the scab

Drowning

In the blood?

Trapped

Did you get out

While I was sleeping?

While I was

Fighting the others?

Maybe a few of you did

But

Not all

Certainly

Not all

Because

The wound

Is very deep

And the scab

Well

The scab

It is fresh

And

Only

On

The surface

The Shattered Mirror

Do you remember the time

The Beast grabbed your face

When you didn't want to look in the mirror,

And he made you face him,

Stared you down,

Smiled,

And snarled,

Before letting you go?

Do you remember that?

Makes me think of

When after the "incident"

That baseball player

Barked in your ear

At a party

Where was he then?

So bold just a couple weeks before,

And then when I needed him

Nowhere

Only there a couple weeks ago

To smash a mirror

Kick in that big glass window

"Hey what are you doing you can't do that"

Oh I can't, can I?

And you know the rest

…or don't you?

Because we made you forget for so long?

But you remembered eventually

Especially when she published that story

Telling everyone nothing was her fault that night

And you would've done everything anyway

Even if she had listened

Even if she had stayed

When you begged her to

Do you remember?

Do you?

Do you remember that time

The other one took over for hours

And sent her all those photos

Of what you and your friends

And the people in the Facebook groups

Had said about her and her behavior?

Do you remember

What you saw in the mirror

When you were young

And your eyes turned black with hate

And out came the flag and the parade?

Do you remember leaving the stove on *that* night with the boys

The night of unintended consequences?

And you nearly killed yourself with the stove?

Are you sure you were just drunk or did you maybe want to kill yourself?

And then you thought they had found out about *it* because they were angry at you, your father and your sister?

Do you remember that?

Do you?

…or that time, after getting back

You had called the higher ups

But you yourself didn't know

What you had wanted to do

That night

When you cooked that steak

After the столовая

That was dark

Do you remember

Looking into the Black Mirror

As part of the initiation?

Do you remember what the Shadow Glass looked like in the Secret Society in New York?

Do you remember how the Goddess' body looked on the Altar?

Or the mirror in Europe

Vienna

So young and so lithe

Yourself first

Exploring

And then

You and her?

In the hotel in Budapest

With the Unicum

And the concrete

And her smiles?

You were so happy and beautiful and undamaged back then

We wish we could save you

And find you a nice smart cute girl

Who listens to Morrissey

Like Kate

Pale skin dark hair blue eyes

Not too tall or curvy

Not like your others

Sweet, cute, innocent

You could have lived in Slovenia together

Or Wisconsin

Or what about the time at the beach in Montauk

Just enough shrooms

In the tent at night?

When it felt like hard liquid sand?

Don't you miss her?

Do you remember?

Do you?

Or how you fled

When the phalanx came

For the mob

And you just wanted to get away

When the girls calmly walked?

That was embarrassing

But not as bad

As the professor

Who wanted you right away

But you were just too damaged

You could never stop showing them

Could you?

Shoving the wounds in their faces

Trying to engulf them within you

And then the collapse

Total debauchery

Still impotent

Do you remember that?

Do you?

Or maybe that time

Inside the art museum

In Massachusetts

Dark and pale

And bare

Right in the museum?

You had let her be the first

Not that way, but the other way

And then her and her friend

Kicked you out

While watching Crash (1996)?

"You're lucky we let you stay this long"

Do you remember?

Do you?

Do you?

Do you remember?

Not always.

Who can?

But sometimes

Alone by myself

I don't have to remember

…because they're still here

Has he won?

Has he kept all the Kates away?

…only for now

…only…I hope…for now…

Only for now.

Part IV: Путешествия/Journey

Voyage

When I landed

They were studying scrolls

Trying to find

A part

Nobody else had ever read

To show it off

They barely even noticed me

But when they did

They turned on me right away

"Your suit is wrong"

"You breathe too loud"

Any excuse

And then

They went back

To the scrolls

The next room

Had a zoo

They liked

To watch the animals

Tear each other

To

But what you didn't know

Is that

They'd let them loose

On you

Too

When we had that dream

About being inside the cage

Experimented on

By the cold men

In the white coats

When you visited them

Were they studying the scrolls

Or

You?

Next I came

To a petty kingdom

They showed me to the local lady

Her jaw was slack

She was doing

Long division

Incorrectly

I went to the Lord

"How can you put her in charge? She can't even do basic math."

"You won't talk to my lady like that! Off with his head!"

And then

I blasted off

Into the next

Petty kingdom

This one

Was ruled by a woman as well

She held you

Enabled you

Like a mother

"Where would you be in life…"

"Without your enablers?"

Lucky

I didn't have to find out

Until

I did

Because

Eventually

Both of you

Ran out

And what did

She tell me

Anyway

"We like you so much

because you have

nothing else

going on?"

"You think I don't have options?"

But that

Wasn't you

That was

Her

And then

We had to learn

The etiquette

Of sadness

Of panic

Of feigned

Concern

But we were

Never very good at it

Were we?

Not the first time

Not the second time

Not even

Not even

The third

And by

The fourth

You just

Openly enjoyed it

Didn't you?

But by then

We had

No reason

To

Hide

Then

The faraway land

Where you didn't understand

The finer points

The place

Where everyone knows

Their place

Except

For you

That buxom brunette

Or the blonde

But neither one

Thought you knew

Your place

But you did

And that's why

It was so hard

When they took ten for every one

And then demanded

That you give them

The one back

Even your blonde

E X T R A C T E D

But then again

You did the same to her

Didn't you?

Or at least

Tried to

"I can teach you

and then

look at how much more

you'd make in America!"

But in the end

They put you

In

Your

Place

Just like everyone else

And everything else

Over there

Faraway, over the horizon

In the enemy camp

And then

We touched down

On a rocky

Desert world

Traded for a nymph

She put herself

On the leash

For me

But then

She kept tugging at the leash

Demanding we walked her

Even demanding

That you choke her with it

And the leash

Became sandpaper

Rubbing away your skin

Leaving it

Grated

and

Raw

But you

You asked for more

Didn't you?

Never stopping

To think

That maybe

The pain wasn't necessary

But maybe

It was the point

I wanted to take you to the canyon

Walk nude together

But you squirmed away

And left me alone

With the monsoon

And I had to hike it

Alone

But

I made it to the summit

Without you

Backwards

Into the hole

Before the mirages

and strip clubs

and college girls

That party in orbit

You knew

That something

Was in

Your bloodstream

Maybe they could tell

Maybe you just looked tired

Maybe only you

But it was far better

Than that time

On 34th

Foaming at the mouth

They kept dancing

Nobody stopped

Except for a second

To drag away

The body

Was that

Almost me?

No

We just

Teleported

Away

Not like

Our friend

Cash withdrawal

ATM

30%

"Look at

All my poison!"

he proclaimed proudly

"I was just sleeping"

"I was just taking a nap"

"I was.."

The land of the rock people

Was maybe the worst

"Why do you all

Feel so hard

And look so

Murky?

I can't even tell

What you're

Doing."

But the rock people stayed silent.

The rock people didn't move.

I had dealt with rock people before, in my homeland.

But not like this

Not like these

"Why are you so loud? Why are you so soft?" they said

Before crushing me

Between their boulder-hands

The land of the little rock people

Was hardly any better

"I'm 1/8 rock person myself!"

I told them

It didn't matter

"You don't look rock person to me"

And they turned you around

At the border

"But what if I have rock person family?"

"Are they dying?"

"No"

"Then no"

It's fine

I don't like rock people anyway

I don't need to go

To the rock lady show

Or spend my money

In the diamond casinos

When we went

And she poured ooze

All over

But it was better

On the beach

I know you still think

We should've done more

And we should've

It was still good though

Maybe the best time

Of our lives

With her

On the beach

At the edge of the world

We bought whipped cream

But didn't get to use it

And that face she made

When she had to pay

For one thing

Out of a million

That face

And on the bus

Shoving her cousins

Out of the way

In her rude dialect

They barely understood

Petty, no?

Coming back home

The house is empty

The soil is full

Of my dead family

And plants

And pets

We traveled the world

But the hamster

He died

In the cage

While you were gone

And he won't

Be coming back

Первый раз в России

Помнишь ли ты

То лето

Когда она нам сказала

Что у нее, в ней есть другой

Буквально один день до той программы?

Как мы покурили

И ей и её друзьям грозил

Емейлами?

Опять емейлами

Ты дурак блять, конченный

Та профессорша нас обнимала в коридоре

Та фигурная, добрая профессорша

А потом мы постарались быть трезвым

Но бухал на Четвертом Июля?

Всё-таки начал ходить в зал, молодец

Мы сказали

Тому украинскому еврею

«Алкашом был»

«Будешь снова»

А потом мы продали те акции Норильска

Которые мы с ней купили на наше общее будущее

И полетел в Москву

Ну, умно оглядываясь назад

Сегодня, как и твои акции Газпрома—

Ну, ты же знаешь

Но как так мы были одни

Нужно было поехать в аэропорт

В ночь перед полетом

Кто там был с нами

Одни, когда он был закрыт

А потом долгий полет

И мы уехали из Кингс Парка в среду ночью

И приземлились в Москву в пятницу утром?

That British flight attendant

"First time in Russia? My wife is Russian, let's get you drunk before you get there"

Что за рейс

Почему ты здесь?

А, я аспирант и я хочу видеть исторические сайты

«Это мой первый раз в России!»

«Увидишь»

И когда приехал в гостиницу, Отель Будапешт, рано утром, конечно номер не был готов

Где туалет?

Наверху

А потом мы попили и покурили с проститутками, первым делом в России?

Такси, гостиница, сигареты с проститутками блядь

Чё за страна

Мои британские сигареты и американский паспорт поразили её

Она показалась

Младше, более

Невинной и наивной

Других

Работа!

Ушли.

Адаптер в ЦУМе

Наверно по крайней мере пятьдесят долларов

А потом увидел штучку за пятнадцать в машине в отеле?

В магазинчике

«Мне нужна…маленькая, огоная машина»

Мы жестикулировали

«Зажигалка»

Печи не было

Ел сыр с свежим хлебом

Водку выпили

Раз с мишкой Гамми утром перед большим парком

Весело же

Помнишь

Как мы скрывали

Наше серебро

Первыми днями

А потом

Осознали

Что в центре Москвы

Все гораздо богаче нас?

В первом кольце

А я думал

Что я слишком богат

На самом деле

Наивным нищебродом ты там был

Но они-то не узнали

Пригласили вас

В тот дорогой клуб

Под землей

Пятнадцать долларов

За один Лонг Айленд

«Хочешь потанцевать?»

«Что?»

«Хочешь потанцевать?»

«Поработай над своим русским»

Другой американец

Кто проехал сюда мотоциклом

С русской девушкой

Ты не понравился её подруге

Стервой была же

Winston Blues

Probably about 100₽

«У вас есть Беломорканал?»

«Беломора нету»

То свидание

Как мы боялись

Обманщиков

И хотели

Чтоб она тебя

Встретила перед гостиницей?

Смешно же

Как каждый в Москве хочет

Тебя лично

Наебать

Хотя

Конечно же

Ты же иностранец

Тебя наебали

Нас, точнее, особенно тогда

«Мой тезис—про связь между романтизмом и фашизмом»

«Вау!»

«Он утверждает, что все самые талантливые люди пере…пере…»

«Переезжают. Не все»

«АлкашОМ, не алкашЕМ»

Другая

Геймерша

Кинки

Айтишник

Сектор Газа in the other courtyard next to the bar

And she told me about how her parents were aristocrats and how the communists and her neighbors took all of their stuff

Including her grandpa's coat

And her mom had to see a neighbor walking around in the coat every day

And we had to keep from laughing because we were a left communist at the time

And thought it was hilarious

I mean it still is kind of funny, right?

А потом перед рейсом

Лариса

И наши Лонг Айленды

Совсем слишком много

Комбо было

"It's a rap song, 'Это wake and bake'"

Поцелуи

Блондинка

А потом

Рейс задержался

И ты не смог уйти из аэропорта из-за визы

И мы выпили быстро же в туалете

И нам дали

Доступ к роскошному салону?

Безграничный алкоголь

И мы сказали глупости

Как

«О, наши родители украли, а потом дали нам всё, и мы еще украдём у народа»?

Смешно же

И тупой

А потом

Домой

Сразу помнил

Пьяный один в номере

Пельмени в номер и

«И тебе» с чаевыми

Улыбалась

A car has driven into a crowd of counterprotestors in Charlottesville Virginia

У, смотри, Underworld на русском

Resilience

I always admired

How you never gave up

When the rest of them did

So long ago

How stubborn you are

How you keep the old ways

How you keep a difference

How you keep

Yourselves

And I still do

Especially after seeing

What it cost you

The naked limbs of the bridges

Rising from the water

Like the stripped carcass

Of some unholy beast

A mammoth

Or a whale

And I saw

How that river

Where they massacred Jews on ice

Was still full

Of death

And pain

And I heard how the janitor

Still remembered

The bombs on all sides

The American ones

And I saw the monument

You made

To the destruction

How you've held it

Stubbornly

Different

Special

Only

For yourselves

Just like

The shard of that plane

In your museum

Unique

The only one

In the whole world

You have it

For yourselves

On display

Крајишник

Да, ја сам аутономан војвода,

И сам водим војну против божјих врага,

На крајини,

Сада и заувек, тамо и овде,

Али често сам сам,

Скоро увек,

И хтео бих да одмарам,

Али стојим сам на крају,

И вечно сам био ту,

На крају између

Живота и смрти,

Генијалности и лудила,

Богатства и сиромаштва,

Комунизма и фашизма,

Тамо и овде,

На крају.

И водим војну сам,

У пустињи изгнанства,

Ђе се гостим душама,

Сам,

Са својим маскама

И својим оружјем.

Јер, још увек имам сечиво

И осмех.

А ви?

Да ли се још увек смејете?

А ја се смејем.

Неће, неће,

На крају света —

Сам.

Air conditioning to air conditioning

Do you live your life

Air conditioning to air conditioning

Sitting in your SUV

That your husband bought you?

Dubai to Boca

Same SUV, same air conditioning

Why do you tell me

That it's still safe?

What do you think happened

to your neighbor, the famous singer?

Is he still stuck there?

Does he see

the things that they won't let us?

Is he afraid

that the war followed him

from Russia?

Do you ever think

About what the people

Who don't have your lifestyle

Are doing in your homeland?

Do you ever think

That there's more to life

Than your concerts and malls and caviar?

Do you ever think

That there might be something more important

Bigger

Stronger

More lasting

Than your personal pleasure?

No

I know you don't

I know you

Live life flat

Don't see the point

Of four seasons

Or even being outside

Instead

Air conditioning to air conditioning

From Dubai to Boca

Do you feel

Safe?

Did the war

Not follow you?

The world

Will never be safe

Again

You cannot run

You cannot hide

The maw

Gets everyone

Eventually

Even in Dubai

Even in

America

Суржик

I went to the Gaeltacht

Bhí mé ann

Like Nanny

In the cart to Kylemore Abbey

Uibheacha agus bainne

Но я не слышал ирландский там

Слышал я ёбанный суржик блять

И там были даже мусульмане

В маленьких деревнях в Ирландии блять

Ёбанный суржик блять

I went to the Gaeltacht

Bhí mé ann

The pills did nothing

It happened again

And it wasn't like Nanny remembered

When she was speaking Gaelic to me

With Alzheimer's

As a little boy

In that hellish nursing home

For the forgotten

Like your forgotten world

Delivering eggs and milk

To Kylemore Abbey

In the cart

Gach lá

I went to the Gaeltacht

Bhí mé ann

The narrowing bridge

Around the soldiers, journalists, and weaponized diaspora academics

Out in Vermont

I dreamt that Fidel, Che and I were in a car

Leather seating

We were going across a concrete bridge

But it just kept

Getting

Tighter

and

Narrower

Until we reached a point

And couldn't move any further

Your days

Of Hasta la victoria siempre

Passed without a single victory

The Bulge

Would you do it

Would you

Drop the bomb?

«Я бы сбросила»

И я тоже

А теперь

Нам надо жить

В таком мире

So would you do it?

It doesn't even matter

Because it happened anyway

Nobody even consulted you

Why would they?

If you go the equator

And jump

You can almost touch the stars

Because of the bulge

From how fast we're spinning

Do you feel like

A curtain got pulled back

Which wasn't supposed to be

And all saw the wall

Behind the set?

"Everyone knows the wall is behind the set"

Well, I know my wife has fucked other men, too, but…

"If you see or complain about the wall, you're liable to be arrested"

"But it's right there!"

"See, that's what we're trying to avoid"

But we saw behind the curtain anyway

And the director's wife

Was taking it hard

We definitely weren't

Supposed to see that

But even worse

Was the pile

The pile of pulverized infant skulls

Mashed up flesh

Ear necklaces

But even worse—

Worst of all—

The necklaces weren't ours

They were our enemies'

I wore my necklace as a child nervously

"What's wrong with your necklace? Why are there so few ears on it?"

"I've only gotten ten scalps so far…"

Into the locker room

Now I don't wear mine anymore

Except when it's mocked

They're still collecting scalps

More than ever before

But only at the poles

Because if you go to the equator

And climb the tallest mountain

You can jump off into space

Because of the bulge

Because of

How fast

We're spinning

Part V: In space/В космосе

Eris

There is only me

I am the fabric from which you weave

Your illusions of order

And your cloaks of authority

No constants

Are ever given

But me

I am

Infinity

Divided

By zero

I am

The last place

Of pi

And

I am not

Happy

With what

You have been

Doing

Adrift

How many times

Can the bottom fall out

Before you stop even bracing?

Or rather

How far can you

Get swept out to sea

Before you stop trying to

Make it back to shore?

How many times

Can you fall

And get caught

By no one

How many times

Can you pretend

That it means something

When the world

Constantly reminds you

It doesn't?

Do you think

There's a way out

For the people

Trapped

On the other side

Of the glass?

On shore?

I know not

And care not

The tide

Will take us

Where it will

Away from them

Away from

The trap

In orbit

The hole was gnawing

Dragging me down

So I

Blasted off

Instead

Into orbit

Into space

Weightless

No more

Black

Hole

Dragging

Me

Down

Vacuum

Nothing

Nobody

But

Weightless

And I stayed out there

Watching

What happened

To you

And me

On Earth

Sometimes

You may have felt my presence

You may have thought

I was there

But

In fact

I never came back down

I

Stayed

Waiting

and

Watching

Weightless

In the vacuum

Of space

You were

My brother

For so long

We wrecked the world

Together

We pushed the limits

Together

But then I went too far

Finally

And we drifted

Only to come back

When I was breaking

But you

You broke far worse

Than I ever

Could have

Imagined

And then

You blamed me

For being the only one

Who didn't

Lie

And you went away

And they still lied

They still

Avoided confronting you

Even when you were

Halfway around the country

Living

In exile

In Bumfuck

Oklahoma

I always tell people

That they offered to pay

But you

You chose

Death

and

Exile

I know you think

You have it great

Or at least

Tell yourself that

But do you ever remember

Late at night

That you didn't actually have to leave?

But even if you came back...

Would you still be lying?

Failed Re-entry

Which way

Do you like it better

Inside

All of the turbulence

Where they tell you

It's all your fault?

Or would you rather

F L O A T

You know

When you come back in

There's nothing left

For you

Anyway

And

The edges

Are that much

Sharper

So

Why not

Stay out here?

Afloat

Adrift

In orbit

After all

You know damn well

What happened

The last time

We

Came

Down

To

Earth

When you tried to

Cultivate

The soil

And it turned

As empty

As the void

So why not

Stay out there

With my friend

And myself

And silence?

Why not

Stay

Afloat

Adrift

In orbit

The Polish Prime Minister

Said

You have to be careful

Around drowning men

So you don't get pulled in

Yourself

Is it possible

To get pulled in

If you don't even

Offer a hand?

Well

I guess

You found out

Didn't you?

And it followed

Both of us

For years

But I wasn't drowning

I was on fire

And you never

Put it out

So of course

It burned for years

And through your village

And mine

And consumed

Both of us

They saw the light

From the fires that I set

From the ships I sunk

Rogue

It burned so bright

They couldn't ignore it

It sucked them

Just like

The wound

And now I have them down here with me

Crusted over

Stuck with me

Grinning

And you see

You don't need to stay adrift

You don't need to float in orbit

Once you've fixed navigation

And called down the strike

It turns out

The only thing that matters

Is production

Of course

The accountant's mind

Rules more than ever

400 years later

And it swallows all

Metabolizes all

Even me

Even me

But

Maybe

Maybe not

Not my grin

Gearóid Ó Riain is a writer, polyglot, and teacher from Kings Park, NY. He has been published in *The Spectator* and syndicated in *The New York Post*. He also maintains a prolific Substack at gearoidoriain.substack.com. He is currently finishing his second full-length work, a dystopian cli-fi novella. He can be reached at gearoidoriain.org